KT-478-283

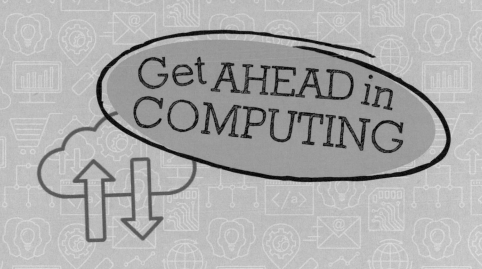

Get AHEAD in COMPUTING

COMPUTING and CODING in the REAL WORLD

Clive Gifford

WAYLAND

First published in 2017 by Wayland
Copyright © Hodder & Stoughton, 2017

Wayland
Carmelite House
50 Victoria Embankment
London EC4Y 0DZ

Wayland Australia
Level 17/207 Kent Street
Sydney, NSW 2000

Produced for Wayland by
White-Thomson Publishing Ltd
+44 (0)843 208 7460
www.wtpub.co.uk

Project Editor: Sonya Newland
Designer: Tim Mayer

A catalogue record for this title is available
from the British Library.

ISBN: 978 1 5263 0401 8

Printed in China

Wayland, part of Hachette Children's Group
and published by Hodder and Stoughton Limited

www.hachette.co.uk

All images courtesy of Shutterstock except:
iStock: p. 20b (ttsz).

While every attempt has been made to clear copyright, should there be any inadvertent
omission this will be rectified in future editions.

Disclaimer: The website addresses (URLs) included in this book were valid at the
time of going to press. However, because of the nature of the Internet, it is possible
that some addresses may have changed, or sites may have changed or closed down
since publication. While the author and publisher regret any inconvenience this may
cause the readers, no responsibility for any such changes can be accepted by either
the author or the publisher.

Note to reader: Words highlighted in bold appear in the Glossary on page 30.
Answers to activities are on page 31.

Contents

Computing All Around Us

Computers were once only used in huge science and military labs. Today, however, computing happens absolutely everywhere and has a huge effect on our daily lives.

Inside guide

Inside your home, dozens of devices and household appliances feature computer technology – from microwave ovens and fridges in your kitchen to the **Bluetooth** speaker and smart TV in your living room. All smartphones, tablets, games consoles and other digital devices rely on computing technology. Much of the music and many TV shows you enjoy have also been created using computers.

The Internet

The Internet is a giant series of computer **networks**. It enables hundreds of millions of computers and other digital devices like tablets and smartphones to all communicate with each other in and out of your home. Whenever you send an email, use social media to share a photo or message, or surf webpages on the **World Wide Web**, you are using the Internet.

Computing is everywhere outside the home, too – from barcode scanners in store checkouts to computer-animated signs and cash-dispensing bank machines. In-car computers help guide cars to their destination. Computer-controlled systems manage lights and other signals to keep traffic flowing smoothly.

TRUE STORY

Poor Predictions! In 1943, the president of IBM, Thomas Watson, said: 'I think there is a world market for maybe five computers.' Thirty-five years later, Ken Olsen, the founder of computing company DEC, said: 'There is no reason anyone would want a computer in their home.' There are now over two billion personal computers around the world, and twice as many smartphones!

UP IN THE AIR

More than 50,000 aircraft fly through the skies above the United States every day. All these planes need to be guided on the right path and at the right height in order to fly and land safely. This job is performed by human air-traffic controllers with the assistance of computers both in the control tower and in the aircraft.

 Customers and computing

Many items you can buy as a customer – from clothing to toys – are designed on a computer, then manufactured using computer-controlled factory machines. Some items will be built by robots, which are also controlled by computers. Even more computing is involved in the item's testing, delivery and when it is sold.

Input and Output

Computers need ways of interacting with the real world. They have to receive information and be able to **output** the results of their work in some way.

Processing is usually performed by the **Central Processing Unit (CPU)**. This is often a **microprocessor** that contains thousands or millions of microscopic electronic circuits. The CPU runs a set of stored instructions called a program. These are made up of lines of code containing commands that the computer can act upon.

INPUT ····▶ PROCESSING ····▶ OUTPUT

STORAGE

FEEDBACK

Information flow

Input is when a computer receives data. The computer then works on the data during the processing stage. The results of the computer's work may be stored and output in a useful form. Sometimes, the output provides information that influences the input stage. This is called **feedback**.

TRUE STORY

Lightning Lines of Code. Some machines need vast amounts of code to run. The F-35 Lightning II aircraft features more than eight million lines of code in its programs, which help fly and navigate this military jet.

6

Input devices

In a home or office computer system, common input devices include a keyboard, a mouse, a document scanner and a webcam. On a smartphone or tablet, a touchscreen, microphone and camera are all input devices that gather information and send it for processing. Devices called **sensors** (see pages 12–13) also provide input on some computer systems.

Output from this iPad tablet are signals sent to the educational robot's motors, instructing them to move the robot's parts.

Output devices

Common output devices include speakers and monitor screens on which text, photos and graphics can be displayed. A printer allows people to obtain a physical copy of the information worked on by a computer. Sometimes, a computer's output sends a series of signals to control electric motors or pumps to move parts of other machines.

On a VR headset game, the output – the game's graphics and action – is projected onto screens inside the headset to give an all-around 3D view.

pascal
c#
perl
ruby
python
javascript
java
c++
ftp
SQL
visual basic
PHP
html
ajax
swift

Computer Languages

Computer coding or programming is performed in a computer language – and just like real languages, there are hundreds of them! Some computer languages, such as Scratch, Kodu and Tynker, are aimed at those learning to program. Others, such as C, Python and C++, are powerful languages that can be used to control major systems and machinery, from traffic-light systems to automated factories.

7

All About Algorithms

Computer programs that control devices contain **algorithms**. These are a series of steps taken or rules followed to solve a problem or perform a certain task. Coders work hard to create accurate algorithms before they start writing program code.

Accurate algorithms

In coding, an algorithm has to have all its steps explained extremely clearly and accurately. It is no good simply telling a computer 'get dressed'. The instructions to get dressed have to be broken down into lots of precise steps. These must also be in the right order. An algorithm for dressing in the morning in which you put on your shoes before you put on your socks simply wouldn't work!

Algorithms coded into digital cameras and smartphone camera apps help the user take clear, sharp, well-lit photographs.

STRETCH YOURSELF

Command a Robot

Link a series of simple steps together to make a robot perform a delivery task, by typing the following address into your web **browser**:

👉 http://play.bbc.co.uk/play/pen/gktkmzxktl

Algorithms are used in navigation devices to find the shortest or quickest route to a destination.

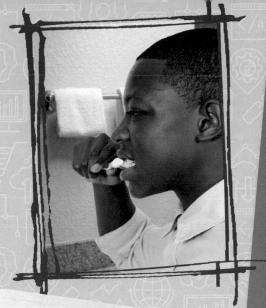

YOU, THE COMPUTER

Algorithms are easier to understand when you realise that you use them every day. Without thinking about it, you perform a long series of steps each morning when you get out of bed before you head off to school, from showering and cleaning your teeth to getting dressed and packing your schoolbag.

TRUE STORY

Costly Error! Mistakes in algorithms and programming can lead to big problems. When a new terminal at London's Heathrow Airport opened in 2008, errors in its baggage-handling computer programs led to more than 500 flights being cancelled and thousands of bags not reaching their destination.

STRETCH YOURSELF

Toast Algorithm

Can you come up with all the steps to make a piece of hot buttered toast and jam? Think of all the steps required, however small, and list them in order.

☞ Have you included getting the jam out of the cupboard?

☞ Did you switch the toaster on?

☞ Did you get a knife before your algorithm said 'butter toast'?

Real-World Algorithms

Algorithms employed by the code in computer programs are at work all around you. They are in the music files you enjoy on your tablet or music player and in smart central-heating controls.

COMPUTER Heroes!

Sergey Brin and **Larry Page** were young computer researchers when they produced the PageRank algorithm in 1996. This rated webpages in order of the number of **hyperlinks** they had to other webpages. The pair developed the Google search engine, which used PageRank and other algorithms. Google is now the world's most popular search engine. In 2016, Brin and Page were ranked the 12th and 13th richest people in the world!

Web search engines use complicated algorithms that search millions of websites for those webpages most relevant to the search words you type in.

Pricing algorithms

Many algorithms are used to automatically price items for sale on the World Wide Web. Companies use algorithms that search through all their competitors' prices so that they can match or beat them. These algorithms gather information about demand for a particular item, and the range of prices it is selling for. Some items' prices are adjusted by computer many times each day.

Shrinking sounds

Every time you listen to MP3 files of music or podcasts, you are hearing algorithms at work. MP3 is the name of an algorithm that reduces the size of a sound file by disregarding sounds in the file that you are unlikely to hear. This can help shrink the file to as little as a tenth of its original size, so you can squeeze more tracks on to your smartphone, tablet or music player.

Heating controls

Smart central-heating controllers make use of code containing algorithms to monitor and adjust room temperatures. Here is a simple algorithm that might be coded into a home heating controller:

1. Check user's required room temperature.
2. Measure actual temperature.
3. Display actual temperature on screen.
4. If temperature is less than required temperature, turn on boiler and radiators.
5. If temperature equals or is more than required temperature, turn off boiler and radiators.

TRUE STORY

Fly High Prices! Two different sellers using different pricing algorithms pushed the price of a book on flies sky high! One algorithm upped the price of the book 27% higher than its competitor. The other algorithm changed the price to almost match the first. So each day the book's price rose until, in 2011, it reached over US$23.6 million on the Amazon.com website! Days later, when the algorithms were corrected, the book's price dropped to US$106.

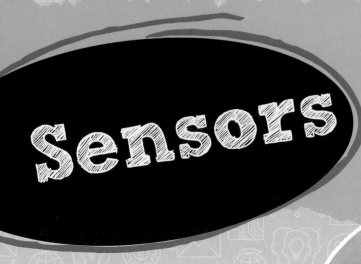
Sensors

Sensors measure something in their surroundings. Many are used in computer-controlled systems to provide vital information that the computer and its programs can act on.

Motion sensor

Security systems

Advanced security systems use many different types of sensor to keep a building or room secure. If any of these sensors are triggered, they send signals to the computer, which may decide to sound an alarm and alert law enforcement or security guards.

Some modern street lights feature sensors which measure how much light is reaching street level. They send back data to the lights' controller, which may adjust how intensely the street lights shine.

Tilt sensors: These measure the angle of an object. Fitted to windows, they can detect if a window which should be closed has been opened.

Motion sensors: Some of these send out thin beams of infrared light. If a beam is broken, by someone moving through it, for example, the sensor will send a signal to the security computer.

Pressure sensors: Placed under rugs or doormats, these can register if something heavy, like an intruder, steps on the mat.

Control panel: This contains the computer that controls the security system, and receives data from the sensors either through cables or wirelessly.

A modern car is packed full of sensors, all feeding back information to the car's computer. Some sensors measure the condition of certain parts, such as the air pressure of the tyres or how the different parts of the brakes or engine are performing.

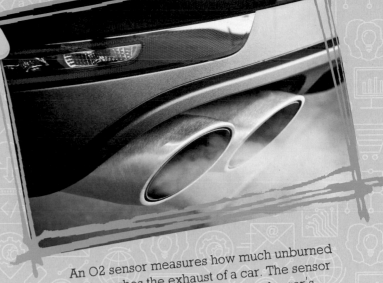

An O2 sensor measures how much unburned fuel reaches the exhaust of a car. The sensor sends back measurements to the car's computer, which might adjust how much fuel it lets into the engine as a result.

Parking sensors

Many motor vehicles are fitted with ultrasonic sensors that detect distances when a car reverses or needs to park in a tight space. The sensor sends out high-pitched sound waves (out of people's hearing range) which bounce off nearby objects. The time it takes for the sound to return is converted into the distance away by the car's computer.

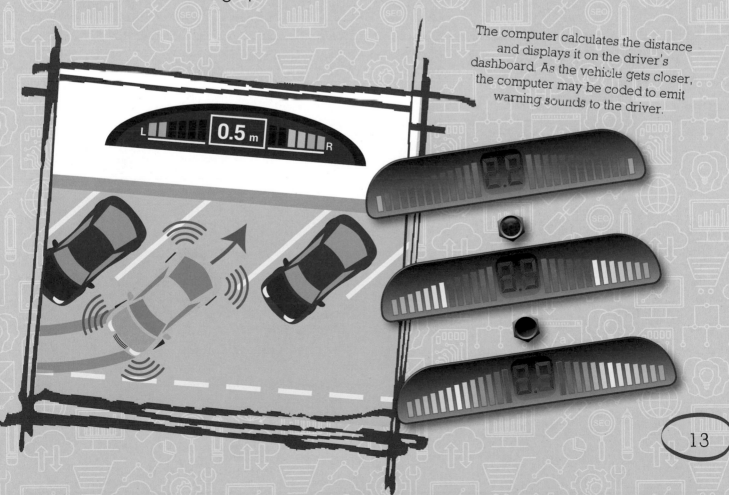

The computer calculates the distance and displays it on the driver's dashboard. As the vehicle gets closer, the computer may be coded to emit warning sounds to the driver.

0.5 m

Coding Decisions

Many tasks in real-world computing require the program to make decisions. It might make these decisions after comparing different pieces of information or in response to input from a human user.

IF statements

IF statements are often used in decisions. IF something is true or occurs, THEN the program will respond in some way. For example, a smart kettle set to heat water to 100°C might have the simple algorithm in its controller:

IF water temperature = 100°C THEN switch off power

IF THEN ELSE

You can add ELSE to an algorithm decision. This acts like the word 'instead', and makes the program do something else if the IF statement is not acted upon. For example:

IF water temperature = 90°C THEN switch off power ELSE continue heating water

Or on a smartphone quiz:

IF answer is correct THEN add one to score and display 'Well Done' ELSE display 'Wrong!' and make raspberry sound

Variables

Programs keep hold of key information in small stores called **variables**. Some real-world computing decisions involve checking whether information entered by the user matches a variable stored in the program.

Here is a simple algorithm to check that a user has typed in the correct password. The password is stored in the program as a variable named Pword.

1. Ask for person to type in their password.
2. Make the typing in become the variable, User.
3. IF User = Pword THEN start program ELSE return to 1.

The ELSE statement means that if what the user types does not match the password held in the memory, the program will go back to the start and request the password again.

Flow Charting

A diagram called a **flow chart** can be useful for mapping out where decisions and steps go in an algorithm. A flow chart consists of different-shaped blocks joined by arrows.

Terminators are the start or end of a program.

Processes are events where something happens, such as two numbers being added together.

Decisions are when a program makes a decision, such as yes or no, or higher or lower.

Input/Outputs are where a program accepts an input from its sensors or a user, or outputs information, such as a message on the screen or a warning sound.

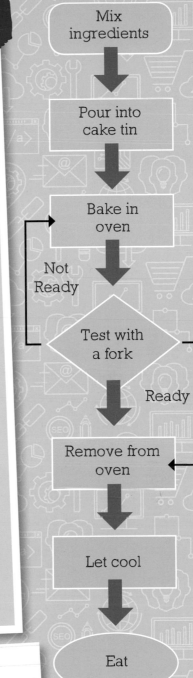

Mix ingredients

Pour into cake tin

Bake in oven

Not Ready

Test with a fork

Ready

Remove from oven

Let cool

Eat

STRETCH YOURSELF

Decision Makers
Can you add a diamond shape containing a decision to the flow chart (right) to check and decide if the cake is cool enough to eat?

15

In Control

Unlike humans, computers never get tired of doing the same task over and over again. This makes them great at controlling events and processes that last all day, every day, such as running machines in factories or sets of traffic lights.

Green-fingered computing

Automated greenhouses keep tabs on plants and growing conditions minute by minute, without human supervision. The greenhouse contains large numbers of sensors which measure the amount of light reaching the plants, as well as the air temperature inside the greenhouse and the amount of moisture in the soil. These act as input devices, collecting data and sending it to the computer.

Computer monitoring

Many computers are at work checking up on other machines or systems 24/7, such as the oil refinery in the picture above. The computer's programs check for faults or issues, and ensure that the systems run smoothly.

The computer monitors data in the greenhouse and controls output devices like water pumps, lights that mimic sunlight, and heaters to control growing conditions inside.

Part of the algorithm for the greenhouse computer would be:

1. Receive input from heat sensor
2. If temperature too cold then send signals to turn on greenhouse heater
3. If temperature too hot then send signals to motors to open windows to let cooler air in
4. Go back to 1 to repeat process

CNC machining

First developed in the 1950s, computer numerical control (CNC) sees computers instruct factory machine tools that cut, drill and shape materials to manufacture products and parts. The CNC's computer contains programs with all the instructions required for the machine to produce the part accurately. CNC machines can run for long spells, producing parts accurately with little or no human supervision.

STRETCH YOURSELF

Car Park Barriers

Some car parks have simple computer control with sensors alerting the computer to raise a barrier each time a car enters or leaves. Write a simple algorithm in plain English to describe the process.

☞ Can your algorithm decide whether a car is entering or leaving?

☞ Can you add to your algorithm so that you can keep count of the number of cars in the car park?

Barcodes and Stock Control

Every time you buy something from a shop, coding is at work behind the scenes. Items on sale are all identified with a UPC – a unique product code. These are usually displayed on the product as a series of lines known as a barcode.

 ## Scanning hardware

A barcode scanner can be a handheld machine or fitted into a glass-topped panel at checkouts. A scanner shines a light that bounces off the lines that make up a barcode.

A sensor called a photocell collects the reflected light and a decoder device inside the scanner converts the lines into a 12-digit number – the UPC. A beep usually sounds to indicate that the scan has been successful.

An item is scanned at the checkout. The scanner converts the barcode's black and white lines into numbers. The code number is sent to a central computer, which contains the **database** of all the stock the store sells.

A search through the database matches the barcode to the product and confirms its price. The database stock is updated (one less item in stock).

The price is sent back to the checkout, where it is displayed on screen and a total kept to produce the shopper's bill, which is printed out.

What have we got?

Barcodes help stores know what they have sold and what stock (how many items) they have left. They are also used to track deliveries of goods and to manage **inventories** in warehouses and factories. This allows companies to keep track of where items are and how many they have left. Many libraries also use scanning for checking books in and out.

STRETCH YOURSELF

Create a Code

If you or your family have a website, you can create your own QR code which, when scanned by a tablet or smartphone, will open that webpage in the device's browser. Head to:

 http://www.qr-code-generator.com/

Type in your website or webpage address and click on the Create QR code button. Your very own code will appear on the right for you to download.

COMPUTER Hero!

Before they had even used a computer, two young men devised the barcode system. **Bernard Silver** and **Joseph Woodland** came up with the idea after drawing lines in the sand in Florida in 1949. However, the first barcoded item — a pack of chewing gum — was not sold until 1974.

QR CODES

Quick response (QR) codes are square codes that can hold much more information than a standard barcode. A QR code can be read using just a smartphone's camera and a free app. Some QR codes contain a website address as a hyperlink. This means that scanning the code with a smartphone calls up the webpage in the phone's web browser.

Where Am I?

Coding is at work in many computers and other devices that help people and machines locate where they are or how far they have travelled. Some plot the best way to reach a final destination.

 ## Fitness trackers

Wrist-worn fitness trackers measure the number of steps you make, using some clever computation. Sensors called accelerometers use the way your arm swings and your body tilts as you move to measure the distance and direction travelled. Code in the fitness tracker disregards small movements but converts others into the number of steps taken and the overall distance covered.

The receiver's code measures the amount of time it takes for each satellite's signal to reach the receiver, and converts it to the distance. By knowing the distance away from three or more satellites, the receiver can display its location to within a few metres.

 ## Global Positioning System

Satellites orbiting 20,200 kilometres above Earth provide round-the-clock navigation on the planet's surface known as the **Global Positioning System (GPS)**. GPS receivers on Earth contain microprocessors. These are programmed to seek out and receive radio signals sent from a number of satellites at the same time.

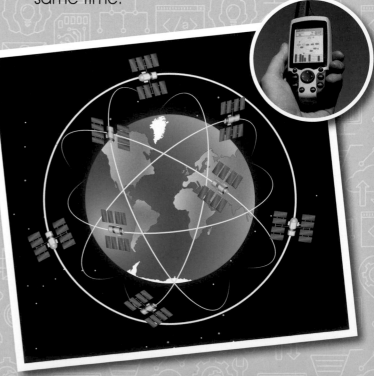

GPS uses

GPS receivers are found in motor vehicles, boats, some smartphones and in wearable GPS devices worn by hikers, skiers and runners. Wildlife researchers fit miniature GPS devices to track the movements of some birds and animals to learn more about their travels and behaviour.

Mapping a journey

Mapping programs use GPS to place a person or vehicle's current position on maps stored in the memory. These update as the person or vehicle moves. Such programs also use algorithms to plot the shortest path (in either time or distance) from where the user is to their final destination.

Shortest path

One method of calculating the shortest path used by computers is to split up all the potential routes into different points along the way, called **nodes** (the circles in the diagram below) connected by links (the lines). There may be hundreds or thousands of nodes on a route. Computer algorithms use different techniques to select the best nodes to travel to along the way, based on time taken or distance covered.

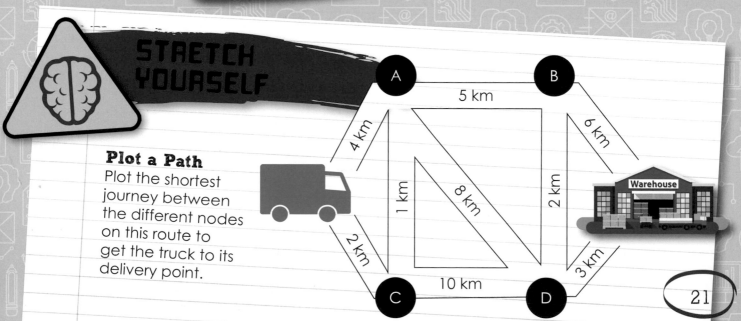

STRETCH YOURSELF

Plot a Path
Plot the shortest journey between the different nodes on this route to get the truck to its delivery point.

A — 5 km — B
4 km
6 km
1 km
8 km
2 km
2 km
10 km
3 km
C — D
Warehouse

Money Matters

Less than 15% of all the money in the world is actually cash – physical coins and banknotes. The rest is electronic and constantly flowing between computers all around the world.

Cash dispenser

Every time someone visits an ATM (automated teller machine), or cash dispenser, they are converting some of the money in their bank account into cash. The bank card they put in the machine has a magnetic strip that contains the user's bank account details. When they insert the card, the ATM is programmed to connect to the bank's computer network to send and receive data and instructions.

Card is read by magnetic reader inside machine, which converts data into signals.

Signals carrying details of card are sent to the bank computer.

X X X X

Once card is recognised, screen displays message asking for PIN. User enters their PIN, which is also sent to the bank computer for checking.

If user asks for receipt, the ATM instructs its small printer to print one.

$ 25

Once details are confirmed, user can request cash, which travels up from the ATM's mini vault on rollers.

The bank's computers contain a database of bank account information. The card details are compared to this. The computer is programmed to decline the transaction if, for example, the card has been reported stolen or if the user requests more money than they have in their account.

 ## Wide Area Network

A bank's network of ATMs and the computers inside its branches form what is called a Wide Area Network (WAN). They are all connected to a central computer or set of computers, and must be coded accurately so that all machines can communicate with one another.

CONTACTLESS CARDS

New bank cards allow people to pay for goods just by placing their card close to a card reader. This is coded to send out radio signals over a short distance when a transaction is about to be made.

Loop of copper wire inside the contactless card acts as a radio antenna, picking up the signals.

Contactless card's microchip holds user's account details, which are sent to card reader.

Card reader is programmed to send details to a computer, which confirms bank details and makes the payment.

Working with Robots

Robots are programmable machines. Some can explore places humans cannot get to, perform work too precise or tough for humans, or carry out repeated tasks without tiring.

 ## Key parts

All robots have sensors that gather information about the robot or its surroundings. This data is sent to the robot's computer, known as a **controller**. The controller's code makes decisions based on the information from the sensors. It instructs other parts of the robot to move or work in some way.

Sensors in a robot vacuum cleaner alert their controller that an obstacle is in the way. The controller's program can then plot a new path around the room.

 ## Control and code

Robots without their programs are far from smart! They require programming in order to function. Many robot controllers are reprogrammable, so that the entire robot can be instructed to perform different sets of tasks after new code is uploaded.

TRUE STORY

Rapid Robots! Some robots are amazingly fast and tireless performers. A team of Chinese robot arms, for example, can make all the 4,000 different welds required to build a Haval SUV vehicle body in just 86 seconds!

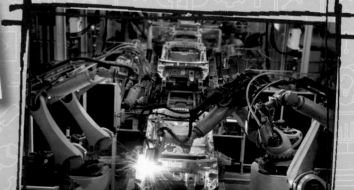

Robot anatomy

The majority of real-life robots are not humanoid (human) in shape. They vary in design, from crawling snakebots that can examine the inside of pipelines to powerful robot arms and wheeled or tracked rovers that explore deserts, hazardous areas or even other planets.

COMPUTER Hero!

George Devol and Joseph Engelberger developed and programmed the first robot that worked for a living. The Unimate was a robot arm put to work handling red-hot metal in a car-making factory in 1961. It managed to work 100,000 hours before it was retired.

Remote control or autonomous?

Some robot-like devices, such as flying drones, are remote-controlled by a human operator who sends commands via a cable or radio signals. Other robots work without human control or supervision once programmed. These are known as autonomous robots.

STRETCH YOURSELF

Design a Robot
Grab some paper and pens and design two of the following three robots:

1. A robot that searches for survivors in fires and collapsed buildings.

2. A lawn-mowing robot.

3. A humanoid robot that greets visitors and shows them around a museum.

Think about the following questions:

☞ What sort of hazards or obstacles would each robot face?

☞ What sort of sensors would each type of robot require?

☞ What sort of algorithms would each robot need to perform its task safely?

3D Printing

A normal printer receives a digital file from a computer and the program code helps turn it into a form that can be output onto paper. **3D** printers perform a similar job, but instead of a two-dimensional (2D) printout, they produce three-dimensional (3D) objects – with height, length and depth.

Layer by layer

3D printers 'print' by applying a thin layer of material, usually a type of plastic stored on spools, like wire. Each layer is often just 0.1 mm thick, so the printer has to print many layers to complete an object.

1 An accurate 3D model is produced on a computer. It is normally created using a **CAD** (computer-aided design) program which allows people to design 3D objects on screen.

2 Sometimes, an additional program called a slicer is needed. This analyses the object and produces code describing the object slice by thin slice. Hundreds or thousands of slices may make up an object.

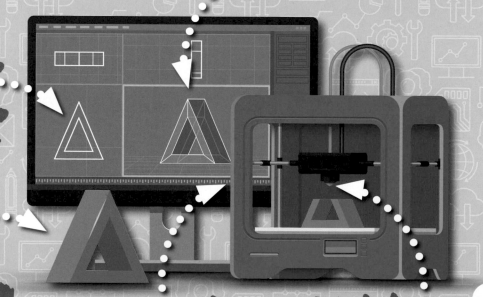

5 The completed object is exactly the same shape as the digital model stored on the computer.

3 The final file is sent to the 3D printer. The file contains code which instructs the printer about what it should print for each layer.

4 The 3D printer's head passes over the object many times, building it up layer by layer. A large or complex object can take many hours of printing.

RAPID PROTOTYPING

3D printers were invented in the 1980s, but it is only in the last ten years that their use has really boomed. One of their most important uses is called rapid prototyping. 3D printing allows engineers and inventors to produce early, single versions of their products – called prototypes – speedily and easily and without having to tool up an entire factory.

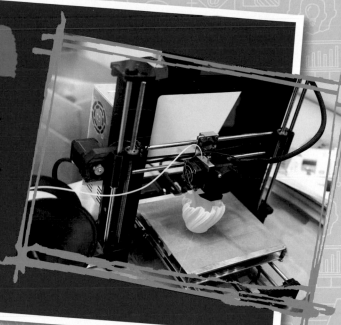

 3D industry

3D printing is already a big industry, producing everything from personalised toys and souvenirs to medical models and human body parts such as false teeth and artificial hands.

It is increasingly used for creating parts for vehicles and other machines. The new Airbus A350 WXB airlincr, for example, contains more than 1,000 3D-printed parts.

A model of a human spine produced by a 3D printer.

TRUE STORY

Print Your Own Car! US motor company Local Motors produced an electric car whose entire body was printed out of plastic strengthened with carbon fibres. The Strati took 44 hours to print on a giant 3D printer. It can travel over 180 km before its batteries need recharging.

27

The Internet of Things

As more and more devices are made containing computer technology, coding is generated to connect them. Many devices link via the Internet. They can be programmed to share information and may be controlled by each other or human users. All these connected devices are known together as the Internet of Things.

Intelligent appliances

All sorts of household appliances can be coded to communicate with other devices, often using **WiFi**. Some washing machines, for example, link to the owner's smartphone to send them a message that the wash cycle is completed. New Internet-enabled fridges use cameras to keep track of objects stored inside. They can add missing items to an electronic shopping list as well as alert the owner when food is out of date!

Connected highways

Roads where the signs and sensors are all connected to the Internet let vehicles share information, as well as managing the traffic flow. Authorities can quickly alert vehicles to roadworks or accidents ahead and can alter traffic lights and signals to let emergency vehicles through to reach their destination rapidly.

Street smart

Outside of the home, many other devices are being coded to connect to the Internet and exchange information in useful ways. Street lights, for example, can send back data to a repair centre when they need fixing or bulbs replacing. Smart bins can alert waste collectors when they need emptying.

SMART HOMES

Linked together, a number of devices can form a smart home. A smart home's lights, heating and cooling, and many other features can be controlled by a single program running on a tablet or other digital device.

Sensors can detect everyone has gone to bed and switch off all spare lighting to save energy.

Smart ovens can be instructed to turn on and warm up by smart fridge.

Security systems can send outside views of the home to the TV or tablet, or instruct all lights to come on.

Digital assistant can recognise a person's voice and detail their reminders and to-do lists.

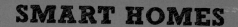

Missing keys tagged with radio transmitters can be searched for, using the control tablet.

Music or radio can be programmed to come on in different rooms at different times.

Users can control their TV and record programmes via their tablet or smartphone.

Glossary

3D Describing an object that has, or appears to have, three dimensions: length (width), depth and height.

algorithm A set of steps that are followed in order to solve a problem or perform a task.

Bluetooth A wireless technology that allows computers and other devices to communicate with each other using radio signals.

browser A type of program used by people to view websites on the World Wide Web.

CAD Short for Computer-Aided Design, these are programs used to create complete models, usually buildings, structures and mechanical parts.

Central Processing Unit (CPU) A microprocessor that contains thousands of microscopic electronic circuits.

controller The part of a computer that receives information from the sensors and instructs the other parts of the device.

database A type of computer program that allows people to store large amounts of information and perform searches, matches and retrieve information easily.

feedback Information obtained from the output of a computer that influences the input stage.

flow chart A type of diagram that maps out the actions and decisions that occur within a computer program.

Global Positioning System (GPS) A navigation system using satellites orbiting Earth to provide precise locations.

hyperlink A word, phrase or image on a web page which, when clicked on, allows the user to jump to a new webpage or a different website.

input Adding data or a command into a program or computer system.

inventory A complete list of items, such as goods in stock or the contents of a building.

microprocessor A complete computing unit on a single chip, which can perform thousands or even millions of operations every second.

network Two or more computers or digital devices linked together in some way so that they can communicate with one another.

node A point on a plotted route, linked with lines.

output The results of a computer's work on data that has been input.

sensor A device that detects or measures something in its environment, such as sound or temperature, and sends back data to a computer.

variable A place for storing data in a computer program, which can be changed by other parts of the program's code.

WiFi Wireless network technology that allows people to connect computers and other digital devices to each other and the Internet.

World Wide Web A collection of information that can be accessed by the Internet.

Books

I'm an App Developer (Generation Code)
by Max Wainewright (Wayland, 2017)

Computing & Programming (Quick Experts' Guide)
by Shahneila Saeed (Wayland, 2016)

A Robot World by Clive Gifford (Franklin Watts, 2017)

Today's Technology (Infographic How It Works)
by Jon Richards and Ed Simkins (Wayland, 2016)

Websites

http://www.whatisaqrcode.co.uk/
Learn more about QR codes and what they can do at this handy webpage.

http://www.bbc.co.uk/schools/gcsebitesize/design/
systemscontrol/workingwithsystemsrev4.shtml
See the algorithm and decision making required for a car park barrier to operate.

https://code.org/curriculum/unplugged
Check out this fun and informative collection of activities to learn more about programming.

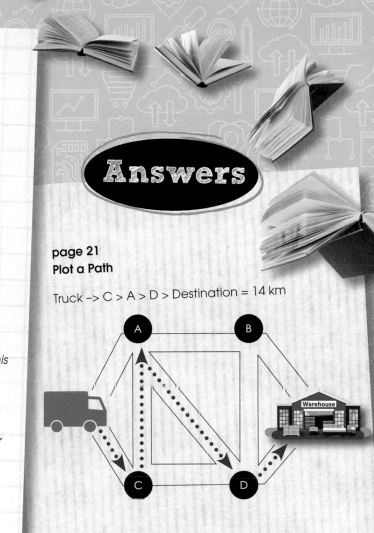

Answers

page 21
Plot a Path

Truck –> C > A > D > Destination = 14 km

Index

TITLES IN THE SERIES

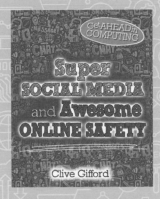

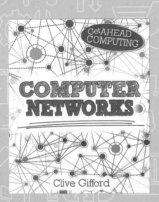